LOVE TASTY INDIAN FOOD? HATE THE CALORIES?

Healthy & Simple: Indian Inspired Recipes

UnderDog Chefs

CONTENTS

ACKNOWLEDGE-MENTS

Dear Reader,

Thank you for the opportunity,

UnderDog Chefs

INTRODUCTION

Who is this book for?

This recipe book is for people who have a love for cooking Indian food, but would like it to be healthier, easier to prepare and cook. But most of all it's for people who like to eat tasty food with freedom and without having to feel guilty about the amount of calories it contains. If that's you then read on.

What this book is not?

This book recipe won't take you through the long history of the origins of Indian food and how it has evolved over time. You can read up on that in many other places when you have free time.

Also, the focus is not to provide authentic Indian recipes, but unique dishes inspired by Indian cuisine. We're lucky to have so many more ingredients available, so why not experiment and experience something new.

Overall, the objective is to keep it healthy and simple by providing to the point recipes that don't require any specialist kitchen equipment.

Why are our recipes healthier?

The recipes in this book seek to be healthier by:

❖ **Using less fat** - you'll be surprised that you don't have to use copious amounts of cooking oils and fats to make great tasting Indian food. Using non-stick pots and pans and strategic cooking practices reduce the need for so much grease. See the Equipment section for our recommendations.

❖ **Low fat/fat-free alternatives** - where possible the recipes remove or reduce fatty ingredients. This is not taking away all the good stuff or compromising on taste; its simply using less or lower fat alternatives.

❖ **More and/or hidden vegetables** - increasing the use of vegetables not only provides a more balanced diet, but can also help reduce the calorific content of food. Its so easy to do in Indian dishes by hiding them in curry sauces or by adding some meatiness to them; making them much more appetizing.

❖ **The humble chapatti** - most people when eating Indian food opt for an accompaniment of rice or naan which are highly calorific. I encourage the accompaniment of the humble chapatti that is low calorie, filling and more nutritious than the former. Luckily you don't have to learn how to make them as they're readily available in most supermarkets or Indian shops.

What do our recipes cover?

Our recipes cover a range of vegan, vegetarian and meat dishes. This includes snacks, drinks, main meals and dips.

But if you don't cook and eat them you'll never truly know how delicious they are so don't wait - COOK!

SNACKS

POPPADOM CHAAT

Prep Time: 10 mins

Cook Time: 2 mins

Servings: 2

Ingredients

- ❖ 2 x microwavable poppadom
- ❖ 1 salad tomato finely diced
- ❖ 1 x small red onion finely diced
- ❖ 1/4 cucumber finely diced
- ❖ 1/2 handful fresh coriander finely chopped
- ❖ squeeze of lemon/lime juice
- ❖ sprinkle of chaat masala
- ❖ sprinkle of chilli flakes (optional)

Instructions

1. Microwave each poppadom on full power for 1 minute then plate.
2. Combine the red onion, tomato, cucumber and coriander in a bowl and add a squeeze of lemon/lime juice.
3. Break each poppadom into 3-5 pieces and top with the salad mix.
4. Sprinkle with chaat masala to taste.
5. Sprinkle with chilli flakes (optional).
6. Serve with one of our dip recipes.

TANDOORI STYLE CRISPY KING PRAWNS

Prep Time: 15 mins

Cook Time: 10 mins

Servings: 3-4

Ingredients

- ❖ 240g uncooked king peeled king prawns (fresh or defrosted)
- ❖ 2 tablespoons tandoori paste
- ❖ 1 tea spoon tikka paste
- ❖ 2 tea spoons cooking oil
- ❖ 2 tablespoons golden or panko breadcrumbs
- ❖ salt to taste
- ❖ squeeze of lemon juice

Instructions

1. Butterfly each king prawn by scoring the back of it with a small knife and then wash and drain them.
2. Dry the prawns as much as possible with paper towel and put in a mixing bowl.
3. Add the tandoori paste, tikka paste, cooking oil, golden breadcrumbs and salt to taste and mix together to coat the prawns.
4. Pan fry the prawns in a dry shallow non-stick frying pan on a medium heat turning the prawns when one side is golden.

5. When cooked squeeze over some lemon juice.
6. Serve with one of our dip recipes.

CAULI TIKKA BITES

Prep Time: 25 mins

Cook Time: 40 mins

Servings: 3-5

Ingredients

- ❖ 2 cups cauliflower florets
- ❖ 1/2 cup fat-free greek yoghurt
- ❖ 2 table spoons besan/chickpea flour
- ❖ 2 table spoons tikka paste
- ❖ 1 table spoon cooking oil
- ❖ 1/2 tea spoon cumin seeds
- ❖ 1/2 tea spoon garlic powder
- ❖ salt to taste

Instructions

Preheat the oven to 350°F (180°F).

1. Put the cauliflower florets into a mixing bowl.
2. Add the fat-free yoghurt, tikka paste, chickpea flour, cooking oil, cumin seeds, garlic powder and salt to the florets and mix together.
3. Transfer to a lined baking tray and bake for 15-20 minutes and then turn and bake for another 15-12 minutes.
4. Serve with one of our dip recipes.

SOYA POPCORN

Prep Time: 30 mins

Cook Time: 15 mins

Servings: 2

Ingredients

- ❖ 1 cup soya chunks (1 cm size)
- ❖ hot water
- ❖ 1 tea spoon salt
- ❖ 1 table spoon cornflour
- ❖ 1 tea spoon chicken seasoning
- ❖ 1 tea spoon garam masala
- ❖ 1/2 tea spoon smoked paprika
- ❖ 1 tea spoon white pepper
- ❖ 1 tea spoon cooking oil

Instructions

1. Put water in your kettle and put it on to boil.
2. Add the soya chunks to a large bowl.
3. Once the kettle has boiled, pour the hot water over the soya chunks for 30 minutes.
4. Whilst your waiting, in a small bowl mix together the cornflour, chicken seasoning, garam masala, smoked paprika, white pepper and salt to make the spicy coating.
5. After 30 minutes, the soya chunks would have doubled in size. Drain the water and squeeze out any excess liquid using your palms and put the soya chunks in a dry

bowl.

6. Add the spicy coating to the soya chunks and mix together evenly coating each chunk.

7. Add the cooking oil to a non-stick shallow frying pan and bring up to a medium heat.

8. Add the soya chunks to the frying pan and allow to toast, moving them every 2 mins until golden.

9. Turn the heat up to high for 2 mins to slightly char the chunks (optional).

SPICY SWEET POTATO WEDGES

Prep Time: 10 mins

Cook Time: 35 mins

Servings: 4-6

Ingredients

- ❖ 1kg of raw sweet potato, washed, dried and sliced into wedges
- ❖ 1 table spoon dark brown sugar
- ❖ 1 table spoon cooking oil
- ❖ 1 tea spoon curry powder
- ❖ 1/2 table spoon kasoori methi
- ❖ 1/2 tea spoon nigella seeds
- ❖ salt and pepper to taste

Instructions

1. Preheat oven to 350°F (180°F).
2. Wash the sweet potatoes and dry with paper towel.
3. Place the wedges on a paper towel and sprinkle with a little salt to absorb any excess moisture.
4. Combine the dark brown sugar, cooking oil, curry powder, kasoori methi and nigella seeds in a bowl to create a paste.
5. Add the sweet potato to a lined baking tray, pour over the paste and mix to coat.

6. Bake for 15-20 minutes and then turn and bake for another 15-20 minutes until the edges are brown.
7. Serve with one of our dip recipes.

DRINKS

GINGER, CINNAMON & CLOVE TEA

Prep Time: 2 mins

Cook Time: 2 mins

Servings: 1

Ingredients

- ❖ 1 inch long fresh ginger slice
- ❖ 1 clove
- ❖ 1 inch piece of cinnamon stick
- ❖ hot water

Instructions

1. Add water to your kettle and put on to boil.
2. Put the ginger, clove and piece of cinnamon stick into a mug.
3. When the water has boiled, pour it into the mug.
4. Leave to infuse for 2 minutes before drinking.

NIMBU PAANI

Prep Time: 3 mins

Cook Time: 0 mins

Servings: 1

Ingredients

- ❖ 1/2 juice of a lemon
- ❖ 250ml of sugar-free lemonade, or sparkling water, or tap water
- ❖ 2 pinch's of black pepper
- ❖ Black salt or table salt according to taste
- ❖ ice cubes (optional)

Instructions

1. Squeeze the lemon juice into a glass.
2. Add 2 pinch's of ground black pepper.
3. Add ice cubes to preference (optional).
4. Pour in one of the following (cold).
   - sugar-free lemonade
   - sparkling water
   - tap water
5. Add black salt or table salt to taste.
6. Stir all the ingredients well and serve.

MANGO LASSI

Prep Time: 5

Cook Time: 0

Servings: 3

Ingredients

- ❖ 1 cup frozen mango or alphonso mango pulp
- ❖ 1 cup fat-free Greek yoghurt
- ❖ 1 cup ice cubes
- ❖ 2-3 fresh mint leaves
- ❖ pinch of salt
- ❖ 1/4 teaspoon green cardamom powder (optional)
- ❖ sugar to taste (optional)
- ❖ tap water (optional)

Instructions

1. Add the mango, fat-free Greek yoghurt, ice cubes, mint leaves, salt and cardamom powder (optional) to a blender.
2. Blend the mixture until smooth.
3. Check the consistency and sweetness and adjust it with water and sugar to preference.
4. Pour into glasses and serve.

SPICED TEA

Prep Time: 2 mins

Cook Time: 2 mins

Servings: 1

Ingredients

- ❖ 1 regular tea bag
- ❖ 1 green cardamom pod
- ❖ 1 clove
- ❖   1 inch piece of cinnamon stick or 1/2 tea spoon cinnamon powder
- ❖ hot water
- ❖ milk to preference (can use any dairy or plant-based milk)

Instructions

1. Add water to your kettle and put on to boil.
2. Put the teabag, clove and piece of cinnamon stick into a mug.
3. Press the cardamom pod to split it and also put it in the mug.
4. Pour the boiled water into the mug leaving enough space for milk.
5. Allow the ingredients to infuse for 1 minute.
6. Remove the tea bag and all other ingredients. If you like the spice flavour to be stronger then only remove the tea bag.
7. Add milk to your preference serve.

SAVOURY LASSI

Prep Time: 5 mins

Cook Time: 0 mins

Servings: 3

Ingredients

- ❖ 1 cup fat-free Greek yoghurt
- ❖ 1 cup milk (can you dairy or plant=based milk
- ❖ 1 cup ice cubes
- ❖ 1/2 tea spoon black salt
- ❖ 1/2 tea spoon ground black pepper
- ❖ pinch red chilli powder (optional)

Instructions

1. Add the fat-free Greek yoghurt, milk, ice cubes, black salt, black pepper and red chilli powder (optional) to a blender.
2. Blend the mixture until smooth.
3. Check the consistency and adjust it with water to preference.
4. Pour into glasses and serve.

VEG DISHES

BLACK CHICKPEA AUBERGINE & CURRY

Prep Time: 20 mins

Cook Time: 30 mins

Servings: 3-5

Ingredients

- ❖ 1 can of black chickpeas 400g drained, but save the liquid
- ❖ 1 large aubergine (eggplant) finely diced
- ❖ 1 cup hot water
- ❖ 1 medium onion, finely diced
- ❖ 1/2 can of chopped tomatoes 200g
- ❖ 1 tea spoon cooking oil
- ❖ 1/2 green chilli
- ❖ 1 tea spoon ginger paste
- ❖ 1 tea spoon garlic paste
- ❖ 1/2 tea spoon turmeric powder
- ❖ 1/2 tea spoon amchur powder
- ❖ 1/2 tea spoon garam masala
- ❖ 1/2 tea spoon cumin seeds

Instructions

1. Put a non-stick frying pan on a medium heat and add cooking oil.
2. When the oil is slightly smoky add the cumin seeds and brown.

3. Add the onion and sauté until translucent, then add the garlic and ginger paste allow and to slightly brown.
4. Add the tomatoes, aubergine, chilli, amchur powder, garam masala, turmeric powder and salt to taste and combine.
5. Sauté the mixture on a high heat until the liquid is mostly dry and then add the black chickpeas and sauté for another 2-3 minutes.
6. Add the chickpea liquid plus 1 cup of hot water and combine. Then bring to the boil, cover and cook on a medium/low heat for 10 mins.
7. Uncover, turn up the heat to high cook until you get a thick masala.
8. Garnish with chopped coriander and serve with chapattis (low calorie option), naan or boiled rice.

SPICY OKRA

Prep Time: 20 mins

Cook Time: 15 mins

Servings: 2

Ingredients

- ❖ 250g fresh okra
- ❖ 1 medium white onion
- ❖ 1 tomato
- ❖ 1 tea spoon cooking oil
- ❖ 1/2 green chilli
- ❖ 1/2 tea spoon garam masala
- ❖ 1/4 tea spoon turmeric powder
- ❖ 1/4 tea spoon amchur powder
- ❖ salt to taste
- ❖ fat-free Greek yoghurt (optional)

Instructions

1. Wash the okra and dry with paper towel soaking up as much moisture as possible.
2. Cut and discard the cap and bottom of each okra and then slice into 1-2cm pieces.
3. Peel and thinly slice the onion, dice the tomato and then finely chop the green chilli.
4. Add the cooking oil to a shallow frying pan and heat on medium until slightly smoky and then add the onion and fry until translucent.
5. Add the tomato, green chilli, garam masala, turmeric

amchur and combine.

6. Add the okra and mix together, reduce the heat to low and cover for 2-3 minutes to cook through.
7. Uncover, turn up the heat to high and sauté for 2 mins.
8. Turn off the heat, add salt to taste and mix through.
9. Serve with chapattis (low calorie option) naan and a side of plain fat-free Greek yoghurt or our raita recipe.

WHITE CHICKPEA CURRY

Prep Time: 15 mins

Cook Time: 25 mins

Servings: 3-5

Ingredients

- ❖ 1 can of white chickpeas 400g drained, but save the liquid
- ❖ 1 cup hot water
- ❖ 1 medium onion, finely diced
- ❖ 1/2 can of chopped tomatoes 200g
- ❖ 1 tea spoon cooking oil
- ❖ 1/2 green chilli
- ❖ 1 tea spoon ginger paste
- ❖ 1 tea spoon garlic paste
- ❖ 1/2 tea spoon amchur powder
- ❖ 1/2 tea spoon garam masala
- ❖ 1/2 tea spoon cumin seeds

Instructions

1. Put a non-stick frying pan on a medium heat and add cooking oil.
2. When the oil is slightly smoky add the cumin seeds and brown.
3. Add the onion and sauté until translucent, then add the garlic and ginger paste allow to slightly brown.

4. Add the tomatoes, chilli, amchur powder, garam masala and salt to taste and combine.
5. Sauté the mixture on a high heat until the liquid is mostly dry and then add the chickpeas and sauté for another 2-3 minutes.
6. Add the chickpea liquid plus 1 cup of hot water and combine. Then bring to the boil, cover and cook on a medium/low heat for 5 mins.
7. Uncover and crush some of the chickpeas with the back of the mixing spoon to thicken the sauce.
8. If the sauce is too thin then return the heat to high to thicken it.
9. Garnish with chopped coriander and serve with chapattis (low calorie option), naan or boiled rice.

ALOO METHI

Prep Time: 10 mins

Cook Time: 35 mins

Servings: 3-4

Ingredients

- ❖ 1 pack frozen methi (300g) defrosted
- ❖ 2 medium sized potatoes washed, dried and diced into 1 inch size cubes
- ❖ 1/4 green chilli
- ❖ salt and pepper to taste
- ❖ 2 tea spoons cooking oil
- ❖ fat-free Greek yoghurt

Instructions

1. Preheat oven to 350°F (180°C).
2. Add the potato cubes into a lined baking tray, add 1 tea spoon oil and salt and pepper to taste.
3. Bake for 30 minutes, turning half way through.
4. Whilst potato cubes are baking, add 1 teaspoon cooking oil to a shallow non-stick frying pan and heat on medium until slightly smoky.
5. Add the defrosted methi, salt and pepper to taste and sauté until the liquid dries out.
6. Finely chop the green chilli add it to the methi and sauté for another 2-3 minutes.
7. Reduce to a low heat, add the potato cubes when cooked through and golden, then combine.

8. Serve with chapati (low calorie option) naan and a side of plain fat-free Greek yoghurt or our raita recipe.

SPINACH DAAL

Prep Time: 15 mins

Cook Time: 40 mins

Servings: 4-6

Ingredients

- 1 cup brown lentils rinsed and drained
- small pack baby spinach 240g washed and roughly chopped
- 1/2 can of chopped tomatoes
- 1 tea spoon cooking oil
- 1/2 white onion diced
- 1/2 tea spoon ginger paste
- 1/2 tea spoon garlic paste
- 1/2 tea spoon cumin seeds
- 1/2 green chilli finely chopped
- 1/2 tea spoon garam masala
- 1/2 tea spoon turmeric powder
- 1.5 cups hot water
- salt to taste
- handful fresh coriander finely chopped

Instructions

1. Add the cooking oil to a non-stick pan on medium heat until slightly smoky. Then add the cumin seeds and brown.
2. Add the onion and sauté until translucent and then add the garlic paste and fry until slightly brown.
3. Add the tomatoes, ginger paste, green chilli, garam ma-

sala, turmeric powder and salt to taste. Then turn the heat to high and sauté until the liquid is nearly dry.

4. Add the lentils, spinach and water and bring to a boil. Then reduce the heat to low, cover and cook for 20 minutes.

5. Uncover take out some lentils and press to check they have cooked through. If not, re-cover and cook for another 5 to 10 minutes.

6. If the lentils are cooked but the sauce is too thin, then turn up the heat to high and cook until you get the preferred consistency.

7. Garnish with chopped coriander and serve with chapattis (low calorie option) , naan or boiled rice.

MEAT
DISHES

PORK & ZUCCHINI CURRY

Prep Time: 15 mins

Cook Time: 50 mins

Servings: 3-4

Ingredients

- ❖ 500g pork loin chops, dice to 1 inch pieces
- ❖ 1 large zucchini (courgette) finely diced
- ❖ 1.5 cup hot water
- ❖ 1 medium onion, finely diced
- ❖ 1 can of chopped tomatoes 400g
- ❖ 1 tea spoon cooking oil
- ❖ 1/2 green chilli
- ❖ 1 tea spoon ginger paste
- ❖ 1 tea spoon garlic paste
- ❖ 1/2 tea spoon turmeric powder
- ❖ 1/2 tea spoon garam masala
- ❖ 1/2 tea spoon cumin seeds
- ❖ handful fresh coriander finely chopped

Instructions

1. Put a non-stick frying pan on a medium heat and add cooking oil.
2. When the oil is slightly smoky add the cumin seeds and brown.

3. Add the pork, onion, garlic paste and ginger paste, then sauté on a high heat until the pork is seared.

4. Add the tomatoes, zucchini, chilli, garam masala, turmeric powder and salt to taste and combine.

5. Sauté the mixture on a high heat until the liquid is mostly dry.

6. Add the hot water and combine. Then bring to the boil, cover and cook on a medium/low heat for 30 mins.

7. Uncover, stir and check the pork has softened. If not, recover and cook for another 5 to 10 minutes.

8. When the pork is soft, turn up the heat to high and cook until you get a thick masala.

9. Garnish with chopped coriander and serve with chapati's (low calorie option) , naan or boiled rice.

GINGER & LEMON CHICKEN

Prep Time: 15 mins

Cook Time: 25 mins

Servings: 3-4

Ingredients

- ❖ 500g boneless chick thighs or breasts
- ❖ thumb sized piece of ginger
- ❖ 1/2 juice of a lemon
- ❖ 1/2 green chilli
- ❖ 1 white onion
- ❖ 1 tea spoon cornflour
- ❖ 1 tomato
- ❖ 1 tea spoon garam masala
- ❖ 1 tea spoon cooking oil
- ❖ 1/2 cup tap water
- ❖ 1/2 tea spoon ground black pepper
- ❖ 1 tea spoon garlic paste
- ❖ 1 tea spoon soy sauce
- ❖ salt to taste

Instructions

1. Dice the chicken into 1 inch pieces and the onion to a similar size. Then slice the ginger into thin matchsticks, thinly slice the chilli and cut the tomato into strips.

2. Add the cooking oil to a non-stick pan and heat on medium until slightly smoky.
3. Sear the chicken pieces until golden brown and then remove them from the pan.
4. Add the onions and fry until translucent and then add the garlic paste and fry until golden.
5. Then add the garlic, green chilli, tomato, ginger, garam masala, salt, soy sauce, lemon juice and combine.
6. Add the chicken back and mix together.
7. In a small bowl mix together the water and cornflour and add this to the pan.
8. Reduce the heat, cover and simmer for 10 minutes.
9. Uncover and increase the heat to thicken the sauce (if required).
10. Serve with chapattis (low calorie option), naan or boiled rice.

TURKEY & PEA KEEMA

Prep Time: 10 mins

Cook Time: 30 mins

Servings: 3-4

Ingredients

- ❖ 500g lean turkey mince
- ❖ 1/2 cup frozen peas
- ❖ 1 cup hot water
- ❖ 1 medium onion, finely diced
- ❖ 1 can of chopped tomatoes 400g
- ❖ 1 tea spoon cooking oil
- ❖ 1/2 green chilli
- ❖ 1 tea spoon ginger paste
- ❖ 1 tea spoon garlic paste
- ❖ 1/2 tea spoon turmeric powder
- ❖ 1/2 tea spoon garam masala
- ❖ 1/2 tea spoon cumin seeds
- ❖ handful fresh coriander finely chopped

Instructions

1. Put a non-stick frying pan on a medium heat and add cooking oil.
2. When the oil is slightly smoky add the cumin seeds and brown.
3. Add the turkey mince, onion, garlic paste and ginger paste, then sauté on a high heat until the mince is browned.

4. Add the tomatoes, chilli, garam masala, turmeric powder and salt to taste and combine.

5. Sauté the mixture on a high heat until the liquid is mostly dry and then add the frozen peas.

6. Add the hot water and combine. Then bring to the boil, cover and cook on a medium/low heat for 20 mins.

7. Uncover, turn up the heat to high and cook until you get a thick masala.

8. Garnish with chopped coriander and serve with chapati's (low calorie option), naan or boiled rice.

BACON SAAG

Prep Time: 20 mins

Cook Time: 20 mins

Servings: 3-5

Ingredients

- ❖ 1/2 pack cooking bacon 250g cut into 1cm strips/chunks (smoked or unsmoked)
- ❖ 1 head savoy cabbage quartered, shredded to 1/2 cm thickness (washed and drained)
- ❖ 1 medium white onion thinly sliced
- ❖ 2 cloves garlic thinly slices
- ❖ 1/2 green chilli finely chopped
- ❖ 1/2 tea spoon garam masala
- ❖ salt to taste
- ❖ fat-free Greek yoghurt

Instructions

1. Cut the bacon 1 cm thick strips/chunks and cook in a non-stick pan on a medium heat until browned.
2. Remove the cooked bacon from the pan and leave to drain on a paper towel.
3. Then remove the excess bacon fat from the pan leaving about 1 tea spoon.
4. Add the onion and fry in translucent and then add the garlic and fry until browning on the edges.
5. Turn the heat up to high, add the cabbage and sauté so the cabbage sweats.

6. When the liquid is dry reduce the heat to low, add the bacon, green chilli and garam masala and combine.
7. Cover the pan and cook for 2-3 minutes.
8. Serve with chapattis (low calorie option) naan and a side of plain fat-free Greek yoghurt or our raita recipe.

LAMB & AUBERGINE CURRY

Prep Time: 10 mins

Cook Time: 1 hour

Servings: 3-4

Ingredients

- ❖ 500g diced lamb
- ❖ 1 large aubergine (eggplant) finely diced
- ❖ 2 cups hot water
- ❖ 1 medium onion, finely diced
- ❖ 1 can of chopped tomatoes 400g
- ❖ 1 tea spoon cooking oil
- ❖ 1/2 green chilli
- ❖ 1 tea spoon ginger paste
- ❖ 1 tea spoon garlic paste
- ❖ 1/2 tea spoon turmeric powder
- ❖ 1/2 tea spoon garam masala
- ❖ 1/2 tea spoon cumin seeds
- ❖ 1 tea spoon kasoori methi (dried fenugreek)
- ❖ handful fresh coriander finely chopped

Instructions

1. Put a non-stick frying pan on a medium heat and add cooking oil.
2. When the oil is slightly smoky add the cumin seeds and

brown.

3. Add the lamb, onion, garlic paste and ginger paste, then sauté on a high heat until the lamb is seared.

4. Add the tomatoes, aubergine, chilli, garam masala, turmeric powder and salt to taste and combine.

5. Sauté the mixture on a high heat until the liquid is mostly dry.

6. Add the hot water and combine. Then bring to the boil, cover and cook on a medium/low heat for 40 mins.

7. Uncover, stir and check the lamb has softened. If not, recover and cook for another 5 to 10 minutes.

8. When the lamb is soft turn up the heat to high and cook until you get a thick masala.

9. Garnish with chopped coriander and kasoori methi and serve with chapatti's (low calorie option), naan or boiled rice.

SARDINE CURRY

Prep Time: 5 mins

Cook Time: 20 mins

Servings: 2-3

Ingredients

- ❖ 400g can of sardines/pilchards in tomato sauce
- ❖ 400g can of chopped tomatoes
- ❖ 1 tea spoon ajwain/carom seeds
- ❖ 1 tea spoon cooking oil
- ❖ 1 table spoon garlic paste
- ❖ 1 tea spoon garam masala
- ❖ 1/2 tea spoon turmeric
- ❖ 1/2 green chilli
- ❖ handful fresh coriander finely chopped

Instructions

1. Finely chop the green chilli.
2. Add the cooking oil to a pan and heat on medium until slightly smoky.
3. Add the ajwain/carom seeds and fry until dark brown.
4. Add the garlic paste and allow to brown.
5. Add the chopped tomatoes, garam masala, turmeric powder, salt and green chilli and mix in.
6. Cover and cook for 10 minutes to for the flavours to combine.
7. Uncover and cook on high until the liquid is dry.
8. Add the sardines/pilchards and bring to the boil and

switch off the heat.

9. Garnish with chopped coriander and serve with chapattis (low calorie option) , naan or boiled rice.

DIPS

MINT & CORIANDER CHUTNEY

Prep Time: 5 mins

Cook Time: 0 mins

Servings: 4-6

Ingredients

- ❖ 1/4 cup fresh mint leaves hand shredded
- ❖ 1/4 cup fresh coriander hand shredded
- ❖ 1 salad tomato cut into rough chunks
- ❖ 1/2 small red onion cut into rough chunks
- ❖ 1/2 fresh green chilli
- ❖ 1/2 teaspoon lemon juice
- ❖ salt to taste

Instructions

1. Put the mint leaves, coriander, tomato and onion into a food processor.
2. Then add the green chilli, lemon juice and salt
3. Blitz until you get a course texture.
4. Serve with one of our snack recipes.

CURRY MAYO

Prep Time: 2 mins

Cook Time: 3 mins

Servings: 3-6

Ingredients

- ❖ 1/2 cup low fat mayonnaise
- ❖ 1 tea spoon lemon juice
- ❖ 1 tea spoon curry powder
- ❖ 1/4 tea spoon cumin seeds
- ❖ sprinkle of garam masala

Instructions

1. Toast the cumin seeds in a dry shallow frying pan on a medium heat. Once slightly brown remove from the heat.
2. Add to a bowl the low fat mayonnaise, lemon juice, curry powder and toasted cumin seeds and mix until combined.
3. Sprinkle over garam masala to garnish and serve with one of our snack recipes.

SPICY MANGO SAUCE

Prep Time: 5 mins

Cook Time: 10 mins

Servings: 3-6

Ingredients

- ❖ 1/2 cup mango pulp (alphonso preferably)
- ❖ 2 table spoons sugar
- ❖ 1 table spoon cider vinegar or while vinegar
- ❖ 1/4 tea spoon nigella seeds
- ❖ 1/4 tea spoon curry powder
- ❖ 2 pinches cinnamon powder
- ❖ 2 pinches ground ginger powder
- ❖ red chilli flakes to preference

Instructions

1. Add the nigella seeds to a dry pan and toast on a medium/low heat for 2 mins and then reduce the heat to the lowest setting.
2. Add the mango pulp, vinegar, sugar, curry powder, cinnamon powder, ginger powder and boil.
3. Keep mixing on the boil until the sauce is thick and sticking to the mixing spoon and then remove from the heat.
4. Allow to cool and then sprinkle in and mix red chilli flakes to preference (optional).
5. Serve with one of our snack recipes.

TANDOORI HUMMUS

Prep Time: 10 mins

Cook Time: 0 mins

Servings: 4-6

Ingredients

- ❖ 400g can of white chickpeas washed and drained
- ❖ 1/4 cup fat-free Greek yoghurt
- ❖ 1/4 cup lemon juice
- ❖ 2 table spoons tandoori paste
- ❖ 1 tea spoon garam masala
- ❖ Salt to taste
- ❖ few sprigs fresh coriander finely chopped
- ❖ sprinkle of smoked paprika
- ❖ tap water (optional)
- ❖ carrot and cucumber sticks (optional)

Instructions

1. Put the chickpeas into the food processor.
2. Then add the fat-free Greek yoghurt, lemon juice, tandoori paste, garam masala and salt to taste.
3. Process until a smooth paste forms and add a little water if the consistency is too thick.
4. Transfer to a bowl, sprinkle over smoked paprika.
5. Finely chop a few sprigs of fresh coriander and garnish the hummus.
6. Serve with one of our snack recipes or carrot and cucumber sticks.

COOL SESAME RAITA

Prep Time: 10 mins

Cook Time: 0 mins

Servings: 2-3

Ingredients

- ❖ 1 cup fat-free greek yoghurt
- ❖ handful of mint leaves finely chopped
- ❖ handful of fresh coriander finely chopped
- ❖ 1/4 cucumber finely diced
- ❖ 1/2 tea spoon garam masala
- ❖ sprinkle of chaat masala
- ❖ 1/2 juice of a lemon/lime
- ❖ 2 tea spoons sesame seeds, plus a little extra to garnish
- ❖ 1/2 small red onion finely diced

Instructions

1. Add to a mixing bowl the fat-free Greek yoghurt, lemon juice, coriander, mint leaves, cucumber, onion, garam masala and sesame seeds leaving a little of each out to garnish at the end.
2. Thoroughly mix all ingredients.
3. Transfer to a serving bowl and garnish with the left over ingredients.
4. Sprinkle over the chaat masala.

EQUIPMENT

Click on the links below to see our product recommendations.

- ❖ Food processor
- ❖ Kettle
- ❖ Shallow frying pan
- ❖ Pan/cooking pot
- ❖ Mixing bowls
- ❖ Serving bowls
- ❖ Measuring spoons
- ❖ Mug set
- ❖ Baking tray
- ❖ Mixing spoons
- ❖ Spice box
- ❖ Knife set
- ❖ Colander
- ❖ Chopping board
- ❖ Glasses Set

Printed in Great Britain
by Amazon

74217235R00031